Pebble® Plus

EXPLORE LIFE CYCLES

A Turtle's
Life Cycle

by Mary R. Dunn

CAPSTONE PRESS
a capstone imprint

Pebble Plus is published by Capstone Press,
1710 Roe Crest Drive, North Mankato, Minnesota 56003
www.mycapstone.com

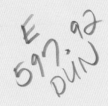

Library of Congress Cataloging-in-Publication Data
Library of Congress Cataloging-in-Publication data is available on the Library of Congress website.
ISBN 978-1-5157-7054-1 (library binding)
ISBN 978-1-5157-7060-2 (paperback)
ISBN 978-1-5157-7066-4 (eBook PDF)

Editorial Credits
Anna Butzer, editor; Kyle Grenz, designer
Wanda Winch, media researcher; Kathy McColley, production specialist

Photo Credits
Alamy Stock Photo: H. Mark Weidman Photography, 21, Robert Hamilton, 13; Dreamstime:
Ondreicka, cover; Getty Images Inc: David A. Northcott, 15, E.R. Degginger, 9; Minden Pictures:
Lynn M. Stone, 11; Shutterstock: Jason Patrick Ross, 1, KatarinaF, turtle silhouettes, Martha Marks,
7, outdoorsports44, back cover, Ryan M. Boulton, 17, 19, ULKASTUDIO, 5

Note to Parents and Teachers

The Explore Life Cycles set supports national science standards related to life science. This book
describes and illustrates the life cycle of turtles. The images support early readers in understanding
the text. The repetition of words and phrases helps early readers learn new words. This book also
introduces early readers to subject-specific vocabulary words, which are defined in the Glossary
section. Early readers may need assistance to read some words and to use the Table of Contents,
Glossary, Read More, Internet Sites, Critical Thinking Questions, and Index sections of the book.

Printed and bound in China.
010408F17

Table of Contents

Turtle Eggs

A box turtle climbs a rock and slides into a pond. Splash! Turtles are reptiles. Shells cover their backs and bellies.

Box turtles live in woodlands
and meadows. Females need
sandy soil for a nest.
They dig many hours to make
a nest for their eggs.

Females lay six to eight eggs.
They cover their eggs with soil.
Soil keeps the eggs warm and
wet until they hatch.

Hatchlings

In about three months, the
turtles hatch. Hatchlings have
an egg tooth on their beaks.
They use it to break their shells open.

Hatchlings can take two or three days to break their shells.
Some hatchlings stay in the nest.
Others crawl away to see the world.

Young Turtles

Hungry young turtles eat during the day. They like worms and slugs. Turtles do not have teeth. They crunch snails and insects with their jaws.

In cold weather turtles cannot find food. They stop eating and their hearts slow down. Many turtles hibernate underground for the winter.

Adult Turtles

Adult box turtles can grow to be 4 to 6 inches (10 to 15 centimeters) long. Many box turtles live to be 50 years old.

Male turtles fertilize the eggs.
Females look for a safe place
to lay their eggs.
The life cycle starts again.

GLOSSARY

beak—the hard front part of a turtle's mouth

egg tooth—a sharp bump on top of an animal's nose or beak, used to break out of an egg

fertilize—to join an egg of a female with a sperm of a male to produce young

hatch—to break out of an egg

hatchling—a young animal that has just come out of its egg

hibernate—to spend winter in a deep sleep; animals hibernate to survive low temperatures and lack of food

insect—a small animal with a hard outer shell, six legs, three body sections, and two antennae

meadow—a big, usually low area of land that is mostly covered with grass

reptile—a cold-blooded animal that breathes air and has a backbone; most reptiles have scales

woodlands—land covered with trees and bushes

READ MORE

Carr, Aaron. *Sea Turtles.* Science Kids: Life Cycles. New York: AV2 by Weigl, 2016.

Marsh, Laura. *Turtles.* National Geographic Kids. Washington, D.C.: National Geographic, 2016

Riggs, Kate. *Sea Turtles.* Amazing Animals. Mankato, Minn: Creative Education, 2015.

INTERNET SITES

FactHound offers a safe, fun way to find Internet sites related to this book. All of the sites on FactHound have been researched by our staff.

Here's all you do:

Visit *www.facthound.com*

Type in this code: 9781515770541

Check out projects, games and lots more at
www.capstonekids.com

CRITICAL THINKING QUESTIONS

1. Why do females cover their eggs with soil?

2. How do turtles know when it is time to hibernate?

3. In the glossary, find a word that tells what turtles like to eat.

INDEX